Needle Crafts 10

RAG RUGS

SEARCH PRESS
Tunbridge Wells

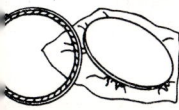

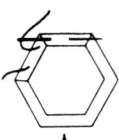

Introduction

Making rugs from rags combines the pleasure of practising a useful craft with creating an article of lasting value. Today, when the recycling of waste products is becoming an urgent necessity, the rag rug is the perfect example of a successful conversion, from unwanted or worn-out garments and fabrics, into a useful, beautiful and hard-wearing floor covering.

Making rag rugs by various methods has been a traditional craft in northern Europe for many generations. In Britain, the technique and design have remained very basic, but in other countries, notably Scandinavia and the United States, the craft has achieved the status of an art form.

Rag rugs are exceedingly cheap to make, they will wear for a lifetime and they are renewable. For example, if an area is burned or stained it is easy to pull out the damaged strips and replace them. Lastly, it is a satisfying and creative hobby for both sexes and all ages.

Apart from making rugs, the same techniques can be used to make hangings, soft furnishings, panels and tote bags, and can also be successfully combined with embroidery and other textile crafts.

This book deals with two traditional methods: hooking and prodding. For both methods you need rags cut into strips, but the techniques and final appearance are very different.

Hooked rugs
Work these from the front, using a kind of sharpened crochet hook to pull strips of fabric through a backing, to make a close texture of little loops. Hooked rugs have a firm, flat and durable surface, they are hard wearing and can be vacuumed as well as cleaned.

You can use various types and sizes of hooks. They are generally about 10 cm to 15 cm (4 in. – 6 in.) long, and have a rounded handle. The rugs illustrated

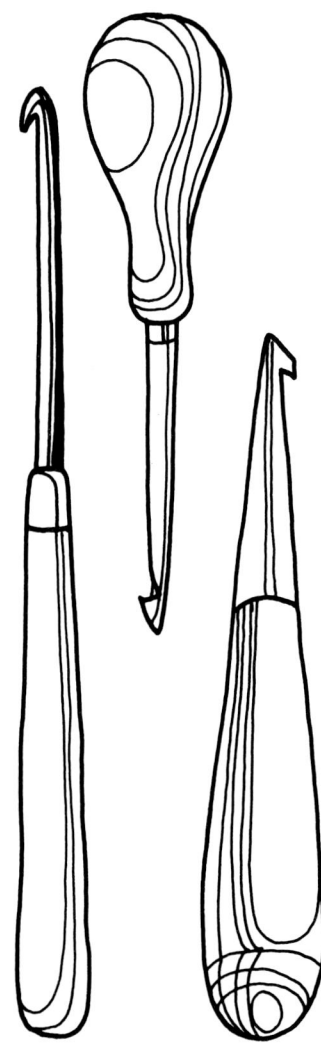

Fig. 1. Various types of rug hooks

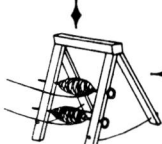

in this book have all been worked with the kind of hooks shown in Fig. 1 which approximate to crochet hook sizes 12 and 10 (metric sizes 2.5 and 3). The size of hook used depends on the thickness of the strips of rag. The hook recommended is shown in Fig. 2 and it is 10 cm (4 in.) long and has a thick handle which fits comfortably into the palm of the hand.

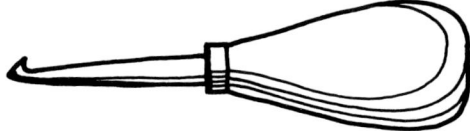

Fig. 2. Recommended hook

Prodded rugs
Work these either from the front or the back. Make a thick pile of cut ends on the right side by pushing strips of rag through the backing with a pointed instrument. See Fig. 3. Only simple designs are possible when using this technique, and they often consist of stripes, marbling or mottling with a variety of colours and textures. Prodded rugs are coarser, thicker and heavier than hooked rugs and are also more difficult to keep clean.

page 4:
Formal flower design. *Made with cut paper shapes and a curved template. Different kinds of woollen fabrics are used, including flannel and plaids, and the pink areas are hand dyed. The colours in the rug are repeated in the border (Ann Virgin).*

page 5:
Random flower design. *Made with single cut paper shapes and worked in flannel and checked wool. The border is made of an old plaid wool dressing gown (Ann Virgin).*

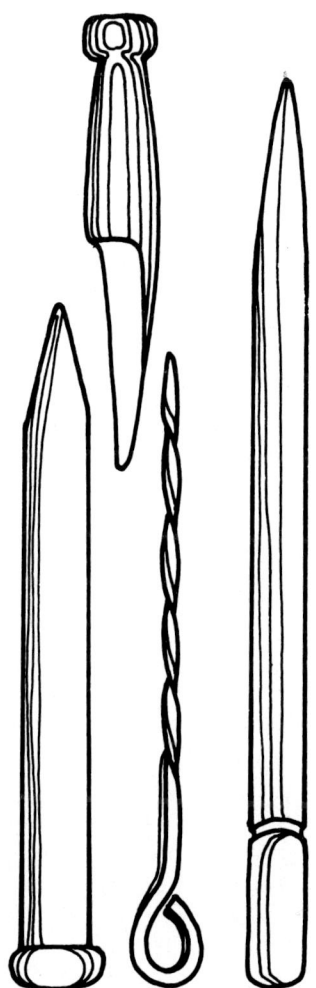

Fig. 3. Various types of prodders

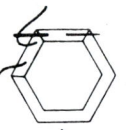

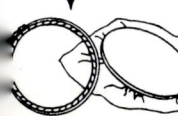
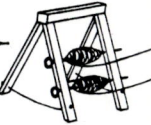

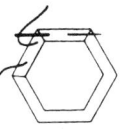

Rags

This term covers all the fabrics used for rag rugs, including old clothing, blankets, bed linen, furnishing materials, off-cuts, remnants and bits and pieces left over from dressmaking.

Collection

Gather as much material as possible: the more varied the textures the more interesting the rug will be. Wool is generally considered to be the best material, as it does not hold the dirt and provides a resilient surface. You can use almost any fabric for prodding, but for hooking do not use velveteen, towelling and hand knitting. In general, do not use any fabric that frays excessively.

Good sources of material are jumble and remnant sales, factory off-cuts (they often advertise), out-of-date pattern books and pieces from dressmakers. Do not discard material with stains, faded spots, burns or moth holes, as you can cut these out. Blankets, flannel garments, dressing gowns and traditional men's underwear are especially prized by rug makers as they are generally of pure wool.

You may need to buy a small amount of new material if you require a particular colour or texture.

Preparation

Cut off the seams, zips, pockets and any worn parts of garments. Tear any large items into strips. Wash the pieces in the washing machine; if woollen material mats and felts, so much the better. Be sure to wash thoroughly any fabric that shows signs of moth. Divide the rags into colour groups and store them in plastic bags, so you can see the range and amount of colour at a glance and the fabrics are already sorted for dyeing.

Dyeing

Dyeing is necessary if you need another colour, or if there is not enough for a particular area. It is particularly useful for backgrounds where you need a lot of one colour, and you can dye many different textures together.

Fabrics to be dyed (unless dyeing a very dark colour) need to be pale to begin with, or in a colour related to the one chosen. For example, if you need a lot of fabric for a green background, a collection of yellow, blue and green fabrics dyed together will come out all shades of green and make an interesting texture.

Use ordinary commercial dyes mixed according to the directions, but do not follow the method too exactly. Tie and crumple the fabrics and do not stir them about too much. The result may be 'bad' dyeing, but it will produce excellent variations of tone and colour which will make your rug look more interesting.

Dye generous amounts of fabric as it is difficult to know exactly how much you require, and it is not easy to match a colour if you need more.

Backing

Traditionally rag rugs were worked on discarded sacks with the seams unpicked. However, this had the disadvantage that except for small sizes, the backing had to be joined. In these days of plastic containers, it is usually necessary to buy a length of jute, hessian, canvas or other fabric.

Choose a foundation fabric which is fairly soft and strong. A closely woven fabric is more difficult to work.

You may use rug canvas as a backing for a hooked rug, but the result is a little coarse. However, the work goes more quickly, the hooking is easier, and you do not need a frame.

Preparing the backing

Cut out the required shape and size, leaving a 5 cm (2 in.) hem all round.

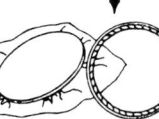

Note. If the rug is to be fitted, or it is an unusual shape, draw the outline on the backing, but do not cut it out until the work is finished.

Mark the horizontal and vertical centre lines of the rug, either by drawing a thread or ruling a line with a waterproof marker.

Method 1. Go round the raw edges with an overcast stitch, or machine them with a zig-zag stitch.

Method 2. Cover the edges with carpet binding. Choose a binding to match the main background and wash it before use.
1. Lay the backing on a flat surface.
2. Lay a strong carpet binding 4 cm (1½ in.) wide flat on the right side round the outer borders of the design.
3. Pin and then stitch it into place on the inner side.
4. Do not mitre the corners, but take a 6.3 mm (¼ in.) tuck on the inner side.
5. Work another row of machine stitching all round, close to the first.
Fig. 4 shows the prepared backing, with centre lines and an overcast edge, and Fig. 5 shows the backing with carpet binding stitched round the edge. When the rug is finished, turn under the binding and slip-stitch it to the back with strong thread.

Frames

If you use a canvas backing, a frame is not necessary. Work prodded rugs in your lap or on a frame. For a really professional hooked rug, use a frame as it produces an even tension and makes hooking quicker.

You can buy special rug frames (in the United States) with a tubular steel structure and wire brushes to hold the backing; however, even the simplest kind of construction will do, such as four pieces of wood fastened together with a joint shown in Fig. 8. Use an old picture frame if it is solid enough, an artist's stretcher or a quilting frame, see Figs. 6, 7, 8 and 9.

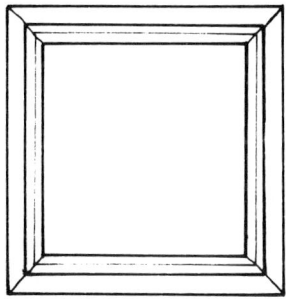

Fig. 6. A picture frame

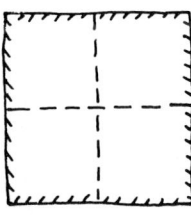

Fig. 4. Prepared backing with overcast edge.

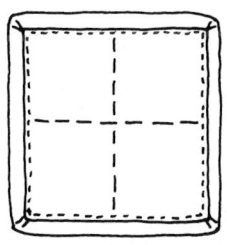

Fig. 5. Prepared backing with bound edge

page 8:
Patchwork design. *Using a large hexagonal template, the first line of hexagons is drawn across the middle, and the rug is worked from the centre outwards. The fabrics are mixed wools, and the edges are whipped in cream Aran wool (Ann Virgin).*

page 9:
Spanish tile design. *The fabrics are flannel, coating and a furry cream fabric (Ann Virgin).*

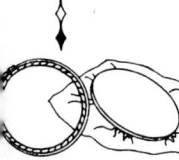

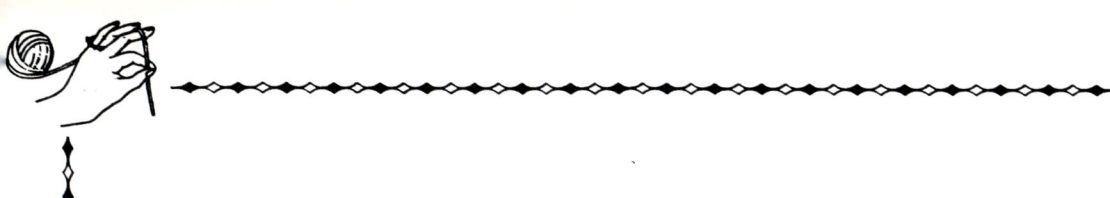
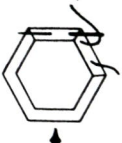

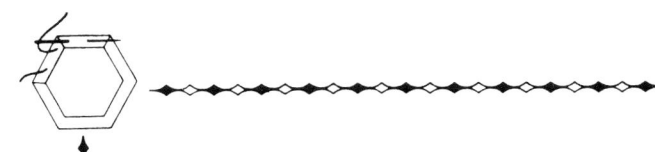

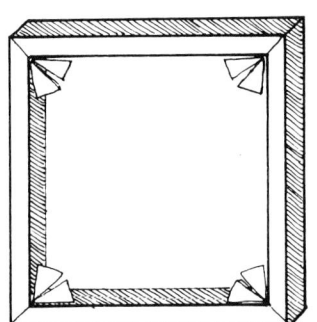

Fig. 7. An artist's stretcher

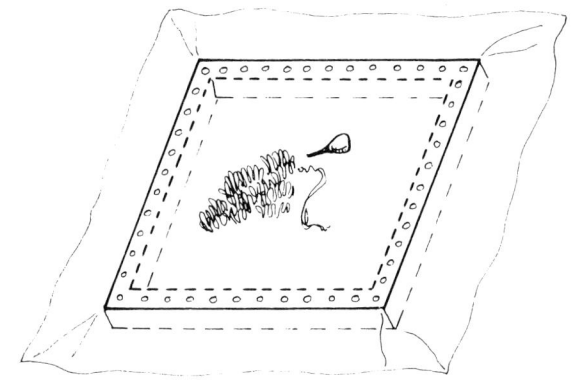

Fig. 9. Backing stretched on a picture frame

Fix the part of the rug to be worked to the frame with tacks, drawing pins or a staple gun. Only one section will be in the frame at a time. If you use a slate frame, roll the surplus fabric at either end. A frame can be propped between the lap and a table, or laid over two chairs.

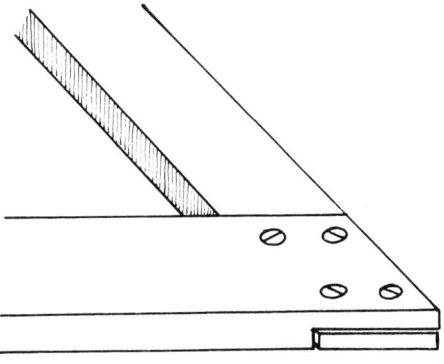

Fig. 8. A corner joint for a home-made frame

Fig. 10. A slate frame laid over two chairs

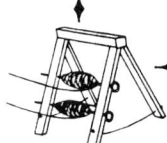

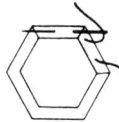

What kind of rug?

Give much thought to the kind of rug you require, as it will last a lifetime. Choosing the size, shape, colour and pattern of your own rug is a great pleasure, and the following sections show in easy steps how this can be done.

Size and shape
Rugs can be made to fit any area. Hearth-rugs, doormats and bedside rugs all have their place, and a circular shape is attractive in an open area or the middle of a room. If you are feeling very energetic, make a fitted rug for a small room, like the fitted bathroom rug in Fig. 11.

If you are a beginner, a rectangular rug is the easiest to design and work, and the most economical.

Smooth or shaggy?
The texture of the rug usually needs to make a contrast with the floor it is lying on. A thick-piled carpet may need a smooth-surfaced rug, a brick floor may need a shaggy rug. You can make smooth hooked rugs in quite complicated and sophisticated designs, whereas shaggy prodded rugs look best in simple designs, or just as a mass of colour with no pattern at all.

Colour
This is always a very personal choice. Neutral colours and black and white go almost anywhere, but it is also exciting to design a rug to go with a specific room.

As a general rule, because rugs are constantly exposed to dirt and hard wear, they are more practical in dark rich colours than in pale and pastel shades, except when used in bedrooms.

Designs

The following suggestions, and the sketches in Figs. 12 to 22 may help you with ideas for your design.

Fig. 11. A fine hooked rug, fitted in a bathroom. It is light coloured in the centre, darker towards the edges and has a border of scrolls (Nora Pearse)

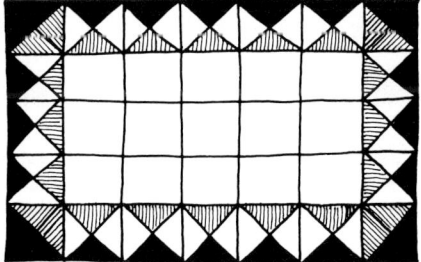

Fig. 12.

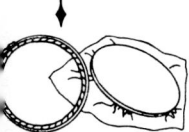

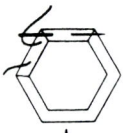

Flower design. *Worked on rug canvas, in home-dyed wools (Ruth Wheeler).*

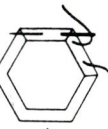

Formal design. *With a flower wreath and a scrolled border. Worked in wools in very fine hooking (Nora Pearse).*

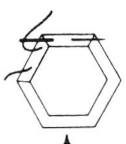

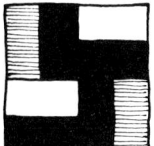

Fig. 13.

Fig. 17.

Fig. 14.

Fig. 18.

Fig. 15.

Fig. 16.

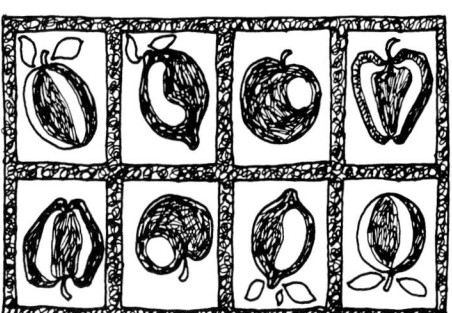

Fig. 19.

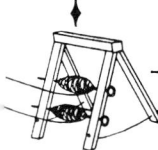

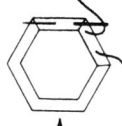

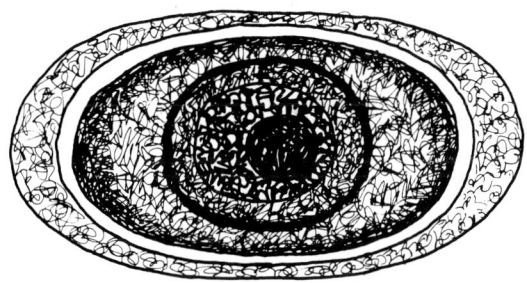

Fig. 20.

Fig. 21.

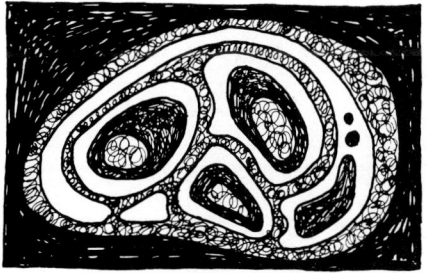

Fig. 22.

Geometric

These are the easiest patterns for beginners. You can make a small rug from 15 cm (6 in.) squares, drawn with a ruler on the backing fabric. If you need a border, then use diagonal lines across the outer squares to make rows of diamonds, as shown in Fig. 12. Other geometric designs are shown in Figs. 13, 14 and 15, which may be combined or repeated, and Fig. 16.

Patchwork

Templates are available in sizes large enough for rugs, so that patterns can be built up in the same way as for needlework. Use a single template to build up a pattern, as for example the 'box' design in Fig. 17, or on the rug photographed on page 8 which is built up from a hexagon.

Flowers and leaves

Draw floral designs freehand, or adapt from such sources as textiles, wallpaper, tea cloths, Numdah rugs, painted china or embroidery transfers. Build up repeating floral designs from full-size paper templates. Enlarge them from small sketches or tracings as explained on page 19. The design in Fig. 18 consists of three circles (drawn round a plate), and three simple leaf shapes.

Although flower shapes may be recognisable, there is no need to make them too real as a rough impression can be very effective.

Scrolls

Scrolls are a traditional motif in hooked rug design, and they make both interesting borders as in Fig. 11 and edgings for central motifs as shown in the rug on page 13. Make them one colour or accentuate them by working veins in a dark colour, outlining them in a medium tone, and filling in the rest with a blending tweed, against a contrasting background.

Fig. 23 shows a couple of simple scroll shapes which can be scaled up as described on page 19, made into paper templates and arranged on the backing as required.

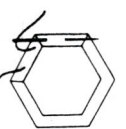

Wallpaper pattern design.
Worked in wools
(Marjorie Kirkpatrick).

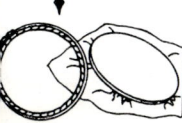

Original design.
Drawn straight on to the backing
and worked in wools
(Marjorie Kirkpatrick).

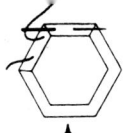

Fig. 23. Simple scroll shapes

Backgrounds

Consider these carefully, especially in terms of tone, i.e., for a dark or light effect. Mid-tones such as greens, browns, rose blues or neutrals are the most successful. Grey is inclined to be difficult, and solid black shows up fluff and lint.

If the pattern is ornate use a plain background. If the pattern is simple, then use a shaded, mottled or mosaic background. Try to avoid too much knitted fabric and plain cottons as they look flat and dull; mix in tweeds and flecked fabrics with the plain ones.

Backgrounds are more interesting if they are varied and if the hooking or prodding is worked in whorls and semi-circles rather than in straight lines (except for very formal designs) and if there are many shades of one colour and different textures.

Further design ideas
Fig. 19 shows a rectangular rug divided into eight squares, each one containing a fruit. Fig. 20 is an oval with shaded areas. Fig. 21 is a traditional design for a hearth-rug, and the bold design on the rug in Fig. 22 was taken from the pattern on a slice of polished stone. First trace the design, then transfer it to squared paper to scale it up. Draw it freehand on to the backing and mark it out in similar squares, as described on page 19.

Borders

These should not be less than one-sixth of the width of the rug. Use a small repeat of the central design, or a geometric pattern. Collect ideas for borders from wallpaper friezes, ribbons, architectural details, and border designs for other crafts like embroidery, pottery and printing.

In general, borders look better if they are darker in colour or tone than the rest of the rug, but be sure to introduce some of the border colour and tone into the central motifs as well, so that the two are linked.

Sketch the design

It is very helpful to have a sketch that shows the finished rug design. Even if the rug is to be striped, a sketch in coloured chalks or crayons is a useful guide to the colours and the width of the stripes and it forms a basis for calculating the necessary amount of each colour. With a repeating motif, complete the sketch with the exact number of repeats to see if the design satisfies you and to work out the arrangement of the colours.

Draw sketches freehand, or make them up from traced motifs taken from books, tiles, wallpaper or whatever source you choose.

Some old rugs, quilts and embroideries are named and dated, which adds greatly to their interest and sentimental value. You might like to find a place in the design to insert your name or initials and the date.

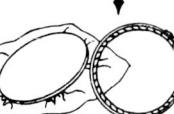

Enlarging and transferring the design

There are various methods of doing this, depending on the type of design. Measure geometric designs and draw directly on to the backing with a ruler and felt pen. Use paper cut-outs for simple motifs. Use a grid to enlarge a design from a tiny sketch and transfer it straight to the backing. Transfer more elaborate designs to graph paper and then scale up.

Use waterproof markers, coloured pencils, grease pencils or crayons to draw the design on the backing.

Make notes about colours and textures. If the backing is marked or scribbled over it will not show on the finished rug, but if you like a neat design, sketch it in chalks and go over it properly in inks when the design is satisfactory. Some people work directly on the backing from a sketch.

If you are working a prodded rug from the back, transfer the design to the back of the fabric. There is no problem if the design is symmetrical, but remember that a free design will appear reversed on the right side.

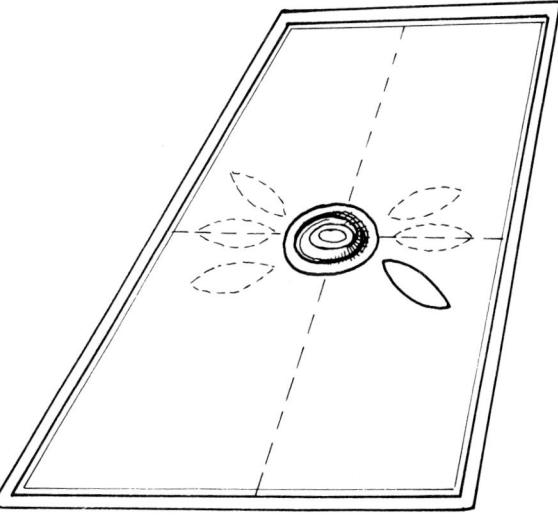

Fig. 24. Transferring the design in Fig. 18 to the backing

Cut-outs

If the design consists of a very simple arrangement of repeating shapes, like the one in Fig. 18, position it by eye Fig. 24.

Draw the central circle round a plate positioned exactly over the point where the horizontal and vertical central lines cross. Draw the other two circles round the plate at an equal distance each side. Cut out the leaf shapes from paper, arrange them on the backing until the result satisfies you, then, pin them in place and draw round them with a felt pen.

If a design consists of a number of repeats of a shape, then cut it out in card and use it as a template, as in patchwork.

Using a grid

This method of enlarging and transferring a sketch is suitable for an all-over design like the one in Fig. 22. It is not a precise method, but quite adequate for simple designs without too much detail.
1. Draw the shape of the proposed rug right round the sketch.
2. Divide the sketch into equal sized squares or rectangles with a pencil and ruler, as in Fig. 25.

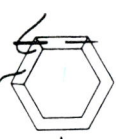

Sunburst design. *Worked in nylon, cotton and wool (Elsie Clark).*

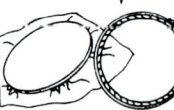

Freely drawn design. *Using nylon and other fabrics*
(Elsie Clarke).

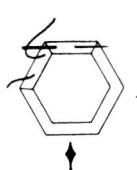

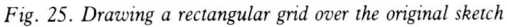
Fig. 25. Drawing a rectangular grid over the original sketch

3. Prepare the backing, then draw the outline of the rug all round just within the hem allowance.

Divide this area into the same number of equal sized squares or rectangles as shown in Figs. 27 and 28. Transfer the design directly to the backing with a felt pen, or mark the ruled lines where the design crosses them and join up the marks, as in Fig. 26

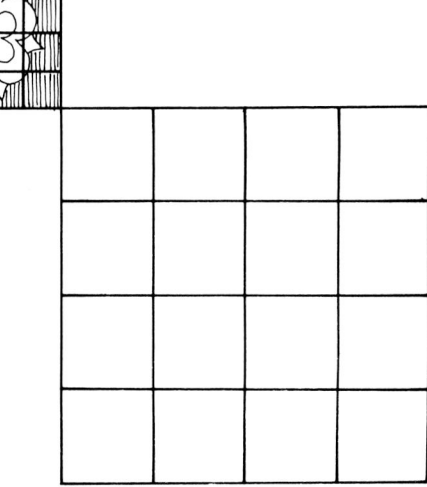
Fig. 27. A square grid

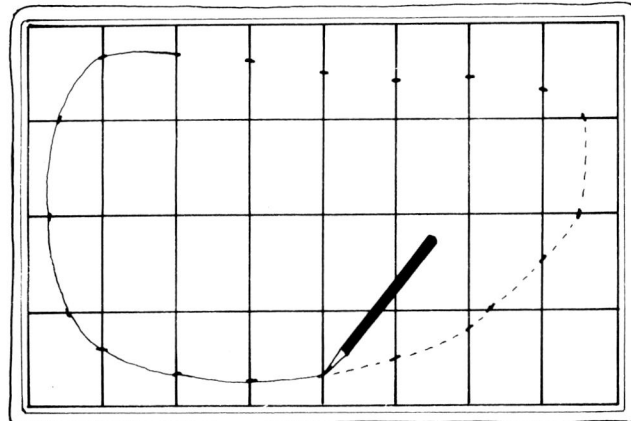
Fig. 26. Transferring the design to the backing

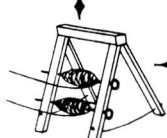

*Fig. 28. The design scaled up into the same
number of squares*

Fig. 29. A sketch of the rug on page 25 (Charis Mostart)

Making a scale drawing

Do this in the same way as the grid, but scale up
more elaborate designs on to graph paper. Then draw
up part of a design or a motif full-size and transfer it
to the backing. The incomplete rug on page 25 was
worked from a scale drawing of the sketch in Fig. 29.
Notice that the design altered slightly as the work
progressed.

Make scale drawings on graph paper. One of the
most useful sizes is 2.5 cm (1 in.) squares, divided
into ten tiny squares each way. Draw the design directly on to the graph paper in the right proportion;
for example, if the finished rug is to be 122 cm × 61
cm (48 in. × 24 in.), make the drawing within 48 by
24 of the tiny squares. Alternatively transfer your
sketch on to graph paper as follows:

1. Trace the sketch, including the boundary line, on
to tracing or greaseproof paper.
2. Turn the tracing paper over, and scribble over the
lines on the back with a soft pencil.
3. Turn the tracing paper the right way up, lay it on
the graph paper and tape it in place. Go over the lines
with a sharp pencil. Lift a corner and look under it
to make sure that all the lines have been transferred
before taking the tracing paper off.
4. Decide on a scale (what size each square represents
on the backing), then draw the sections or motifs
required to fit that scale on another large piece of
graph paper, in the same way as the grid method.
Fig. 30 shows a scale drawing of a quarter of the rug
on page 28.

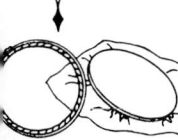

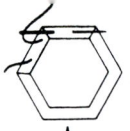

above left;
Sample of prodding. *(Ann Virgin).*

above;
Close-up of prodding. *(Ann Virgin).*

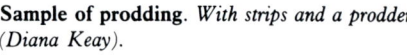
Sample of prodding. *With strips and a prodder (Diana Keay).*

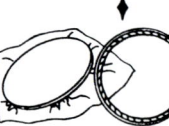

'The Bird Lovers' Rug (*in progress*). *This is being worked from the drawing in Fig. 29, and the design is being adapted as the work progresses (Charis Mostart).*

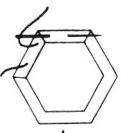

Fig. 30. A scale drawing of a quarter of the rug on page 28 The design was modified in working. (Charis Mostart)

5. Transfer the scaled up drawing to the backing by any of the following methods.

Cut out the motif required, pin it to the backing and draw round it with a waterproof marker. If there are repeating motifs, cut the shape out in thin card.

Lay a piece of carbon paper on the backing, put the drawing in position on top, secure it with pins, drawing pins or self-adhesive tape and trace round the outlines with a hard pencil.

Trace the design on to household greaseproof paper using an embroidery transfer pencil. Make a mark on the same paper with the pencil and try ironing it out on the backing first to determine the right heat. Then place the design in position pencil side down, on to the backing. Secure it so that it will not slip and iron over the design.

Trace the scaled-up quarter of the rug on to nylon net with a felt pen. Lay the net in position on the backing, and draw the design through it with the felt pen. Turn over the net and draw the design through, mirror image, on the other half of the rug. This is the easiest way of all.

Hooking

When you have prepared the backing fabric, transferred the design on to it and framed it if necessary, all that remains is to cut the strips before beginning to hook.

Cutting the strips

Use sharp long-bladed scissors. Fabric strip cutters are available from specialist suppliers in the United States, but they are expensive.

You can cut the strips on the straight of the fabric parallel to the selvedge, or cut in all directions. The only thing to remember is not to use fabrics that fray.

The thinner the strips are cut, the finer the rug. Cut the strips as fine as you can without causing the threads to pull apart. An average width for strips is about 1 cm ($^1/_3$ in.) for hooked rugs and 1.5 cm ($^1/_2$ in.) for prodded rugs. Fine fabrics need to be cut wider than thick ones to achieve the same effect.

You can cut about 30.5 cm (12 in.) of fabric at a time, or cut much longer strips and roll them into a ball. Cut stockings and machine knitted garments round and round in a spiral, or cut straight up to form an attractive rouleau. You can simply tear some fabrics.

Do not cut up all the fabric at once. You may find after working for a while that you wish to change the colours, or the texture. Also, if you cut long lengths it is tempting to go on using them when other colours would be preferable. Cut enough fabric for one work session at a time.

Method

Work either in a frame or in your lap, with the right side of the backing uppermost.

Hold a strip under the backing in one hand, and push the hook through from front to back. Pick up the end of the strip and pull it through to the surface.

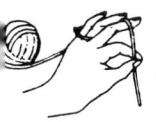

Always bring the ends of the strips through to the front and cut off level with the loops as the work progresses. Hold the hook in the direction in which you are working.

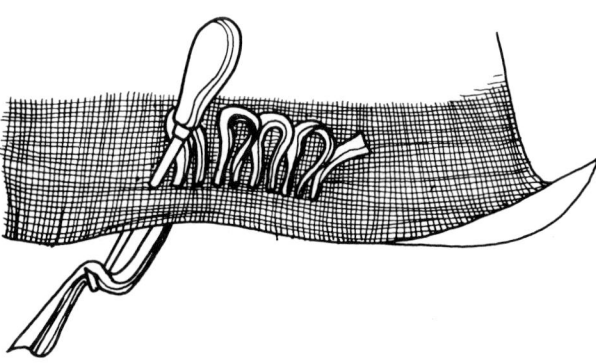

Fig. 31. Hooking

Put the hook through the backing again, about two threads away from the first hole, and bring up a little loop about 6.3 mm (¼ in.) high, controlling the height with the hand underneath the backing. Always make the hook do the work for you by making a big enough hole in the backing to bring the fabric through without a struggle. To avoid catching the backing as well as the strip when pulling the loaded hook through, press the smooth side of the shank against the backing to make the hole bigger.

If you find the previous loops pull out as you work, it may be that you are still holding the strip below the backing instead of letting go when the hook catches it. The strips must lie close and flat on the under-side. Do not cross them underneath, pull the end of the strip up and start another one if necessary.

When starting another row, begin about two threads away from the first row, and stagger the loops so that in each row a loop is opposite a space. Do not pack the loops too tightly as this will cause the rug to 'hump'.

Work away from you, in meandering lines and semi-circles. You can start by outlining all the shapes with a dark colour, but as a general rule start in the centre of the rug and work outwards in all directions.

While working on the rug, leave it on the floor between sessions or overnight, to see what you think of it next day.

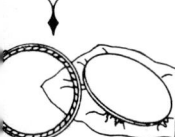

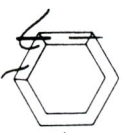

'**The Flower Garden**'. *A design based on the observation of flowers, worked mostly in wool (Charis Mostart)*

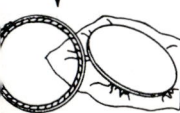

Flower design. *Paper templates were pinned to the backing, then traced round with a felt pen. The fabrics are wool and nylon (Beryl Greenup).*

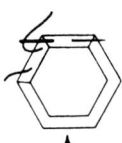
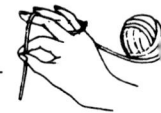

Prodding

Work prodding in your hand from the right side, or in a frame from the wrong side. Depending on which method you use, prepare and frame up the backing.

Cutting strips
Cut a selection of strips about 4 cm × 10 cm (1½ in. × 4in.). This will produce quite a shaggy pile. To achieve a different effect, cut strips in different sizes. Experiment with different widths and lengths to find the one you like.

Method 1. Work this in your hand on the right side of the fabric.
1. Fold the backing, and insert the prodder about 13 mm (½ in.) away from the fold, making a fair-sized hole through the double thickness.

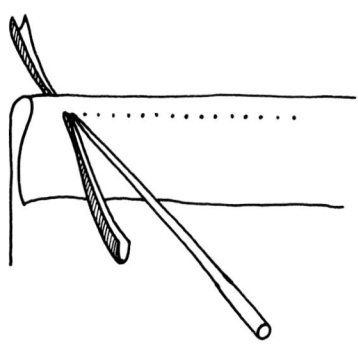

Fig. 33. Stage 2

3. Work a whole row like this, then pull the backing flat. Make the next fold close to the first row, and insert strips across it in the same way as before, leaving about 3 cm (1¼ in.) between the rows.

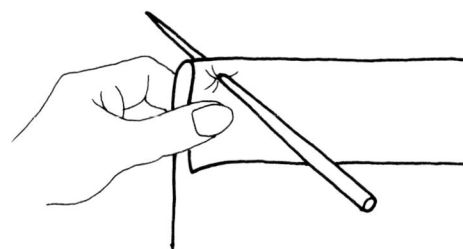

Fig. 32. Prodding, stage 1

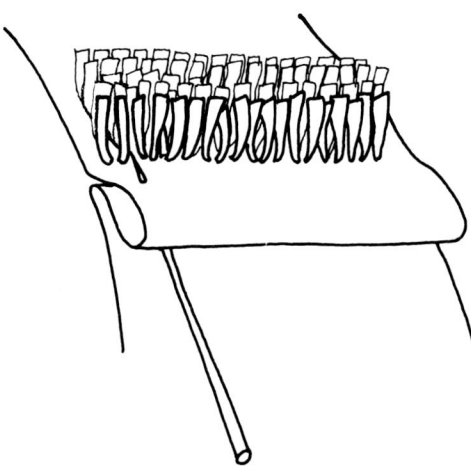

Fig. 34. Stage 3

2. Fold a strip lengthwise, insert it with the prodder through the hole and pull the strip halfway through.

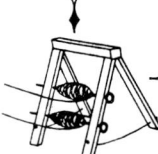

Method 2. Work this on the backing stretched in a frame, from the back.
1. Make a hole in the backing.
2. Prod a strip halfway through.
3. Make another hole next to the first one.
4. Prod the rest of the strip through.

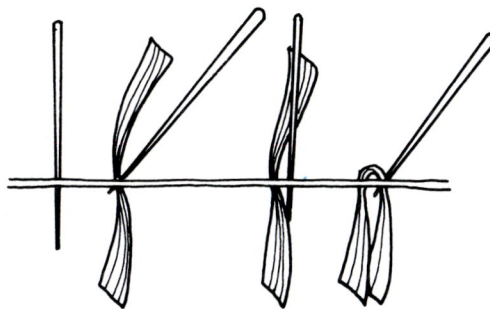

Fig. 35. Prodding, the second method

Finishing

Overcast edge
Turn the fabric over to the back and hem it in place. Cover this edge with another stitched binding for extra strength.

Carpet binding
Turn back the fabric at the second row of stitching, leaving the first row at the edge of the hooking. Sew the binding to the backing, stretching it slightly round the corners. Use a strong buttonhole twine or carpet thread, taking a double stitch every 8 cm (3in.)

Edge stitching
Some very beautiful rugs are finished with a row of canvas stitches, which are worked on the folded edge just where the hooking finishes. Use buttonhole stitch, braid stitch, or edge stitch; the latter is a long-armed cross stitch with an extra stitch in the middle to cover the edge. The yarn is usually carpet wool thrums (the remains of warp from a carpet factory) in a matching colour. After stitching all round the rug, trim the remaining backing and cover the raw edges with carpet binding.

Lining
Do not line a rag rug, or small stones and pins will work their way through the pile, lie against the backing and eventually cut the fabric.

Backing
It is a good idea to cover the back of a rug with latex adhesive. It is not absolutely necessary, but it holds the loops firm and prevents the rug from slipping. Rub in the adhesive all over the back and up to the edge of the binding with the scraper provided, and let it dry.

A professional finish for hooked rugs
Damp the rug all over, and lay it flat on the floor. Cover with an old sheet and a sheet of plastic, and lay flat heavy objects all over the surface. Leave it for a few days. Remove the weights and leave until it is perfectly dry. Alternatively, lay the rug face down, place a damp cloth on it and press lightly with a hot iron.

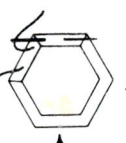

Striped rug. *Worked outwards from the central stripe. The colours were planned in advance and sketched out, and enough fabric for each half of the rug was allocated before starting work. The fabrics are wool and nylon (Beryl Greenup).*

Acknowledgments

Series edited by Kit Pyman

Text by Nora Pearse, Charis Mostart, Beryl Greenup
Diagrams by Jan Messent
Photographs by Search Press Studios

Text, illustrations, arrangement and typography
copyright © Search Press Limited 1980.

First published in Great Britain in 1980 by Search
Press Limited, Wellwood, North Farm Road,
Tunbridge Wells, Kent TN2 3DR

Reprinted 1988, 1990

ISBN 085532 427 9

Made and printed in Spain by A. G. Elkar, S. Coop.
Autonomía, 71 - 48012-Bilbao - Spain

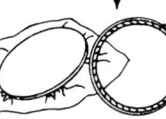